Just the Opposite

Dirty
Clean

Sharon Gordon

New Hanover County Public Library
201 Chestnut Street
Wilmington, NC 28401

My room is dirty.

Now it is clean.

My rug is dirty.

Now it is clean.

My tub is dirty.

Now it is clean.

My table is dirty.

Now it is clean.

My glass is dirty.

Now it is clean.

My floor is dirty.

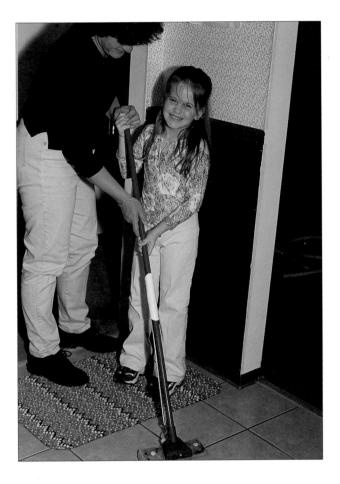

Now it is clean.

My bike is dirty.

Now it is clean.

My dog is dirty.

Now he is clean.

I was clean.

Now I am dirty!

Words We Know

bike

dog

floor

glass

room

rug

table

tub

21

Index

Page numbers in **boldface** are illustrations.

About the Author

Sharon Gordon has written many books for young children. She has also worked as an editor. Sharon and her husband Bruce have three children, Douglas, Katie, and Laura, and one spoiled pooch, Samantha. They live in Midland Park, New Jersey.

With thanks to Nanci Vargus, Ed.D. and Beth Walker Gambro, reading consultants

Benchmark Books
Marshall Cavendish
99 White Plains Road
Tarrytown, New York 10591-9001
www.marshallcavendish.com

Library of Congress Cataloging-in-Publication Data

Gordon, Sharon.
Dirty clean / by Sharon Gordon.
p. cm. — (Bookworms: Just the opposite)
Includes index.
Summary: Everyday examples show how things like a bedroom, a floor, or a dog, go from being dirty to being clean.
ISBN 0-7614-1569-6
1. English language—Synonyms and antonyms—Juvenile literature. [1. English language—Synonyms and antonyms.] I. Title. II. Series: Gordon, Sharon. Bookworms: Just the opposite.

PE1591.G637 2003
428.1—dc21
2003005913

Photo Research by Anne Burns Images

Cover Photos by SWA Photography

All of the photographs used in this book were taken by and used with the permission of SWA Photography.

Series design by Becky Terhune

Printed in China
1 3 5 6 4 2

ML

11/04